On the Train

Paul Humphrey

Photography by Chris Fairclough

W
FRANKLIN WATTS
LONDON · SYDNEY

First published in 2005 by
Franklin Watts
96 Leonard Street
London EC2A 4XD

Franklin Watts Australia
Level 17/207 Kent Street
Sydney NSW 2000

© 2005 Franklin Watts

ISBN 0 7496 6177 1 (hbk)
ISBN 0 7496 6189 5 (pbk)

Dewey classification number: 385

A CIP catalogue record for this book is available
from the British Library.

Planning and production by Discovery Books Limited
Editor: Rachel Tisdale
Designer: Ian Winton
Photography: Chris Fairclough
Series advisors: Diana Bentley MA and Dee Reid MA
Fellows of Oxford Brookes University

The author, packager and publisher would like to thank the
following people for their participation in this book: Bobby,
Alex, Eleanor, Tracy and Nick Ray; Chiltern Railways.

Printed in China

Contents

Safety Notice: It is dangerous to stray onto railway lines as trains travel fast and cannot stop quickly. Always use public footpaths and keep behind the fence and away from platform edges at train stations.

Bobby and his family went to London by train.

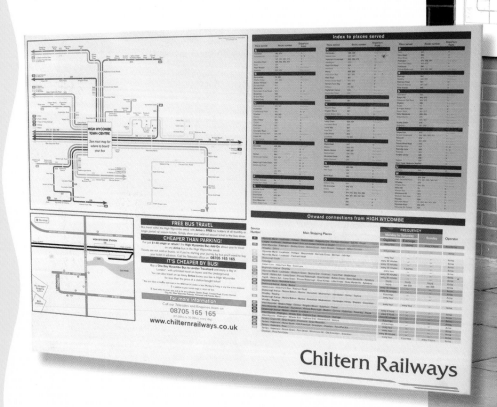

Dad bought the tickets.

The man at the gate checked the tickets.

They got on
the train.

Mum found some seats.

Can I sit by the window?

The train
sped by fields
and farms.

A ticket inspector clipped their tickets.

They ate their
packed lunch.

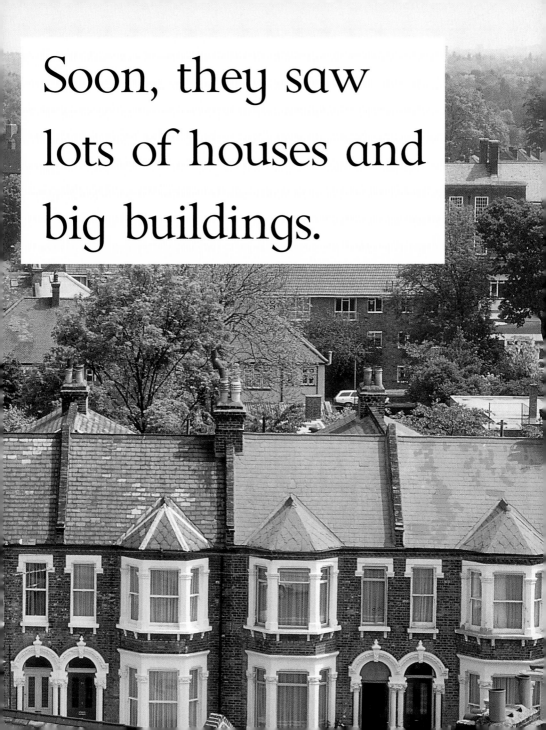

Soon, they saw lots of houses and big buildings.

The train arrived in London.

They saw the London Eye ...

... and went to Trafalgar Square.

Time to get the train home now!

Word bank

Look back for these words and pictures.

Buildings

Farms

Fields

Gate

Inspector

Packed lunch

Tickets

Train

Window